"As publisher of *Rimes of The Ancient Mariner Silver Tongued Devil Anthology: Celebrating five years of outstanding East Village poetry, fiction, memoirs, essays, storytelling, humor, and spoken word*, Linda Kleinbub has not only been around downtown but has embraced the informal savvy-quirky spirit of generosity that is New York. Her first book of poems, *Cover Charge*, maps out dues paid under 'purple galaxies' or in wishful gardens where blessings, if blurry, are bountiful. In the poem, Visibility Unclear, 'fissures of logic' manage to 'avoid tripping over cats' and in Fire Burning, 'Orion's stars drift/ penniless across a/ quartz-colored sky.' Brimming colors mix and match, jiggle vitality. Kleinbub, lyrical, sensual, sober, has arrived, and she's brought with her Pink Trees Press."
— Star Black, author of *The Popular Vote*

"In its imagery, its phrasing, and its probing of our inner selves, *Cover Charge* is truly impressive. Only Linda Kleinbub can make the dirt in a vegetable garden filled with eggplants and praying mantises seem seductive." — R. Bremner, author of *Hungry Words*

"What a great title! All the beauty, the art, the sex, the doubts, the daily chores, the life from subway to sky 'trying to make snow angels at midnight.' Don't you wish you had thought of that line? Linda Kleinbub takes us on a sensory journey from basement to club to the soil, from depths to the planets — clearly a poet with a painter/gardener's gift for replanting and survival — read these poems, and like the canvases and places the 'she' of these poems describes, the images, textures, and colors will live in skin's memory." — eve packer, author of *no mask no talk corona poems 2020–2021*

"Linda Kleinbub's poetry is honest, incisive, and deeply felt. More important, it is direct and accessible. She writes about what it's like to experience life. Each poem provides a moment (or moments) of recognition, when, as readers, we can say, 'Aha' I feel I know this poet better through her poems."
— Thaddeus Rutkowski, author of *Tricks of Light*

COVER CHARGE

More Unbearables Titles from Autonomedia
RON KOLM AND JIM FEAST, SERIES EDITORS

COVER CHARGE

Linda Kleinbub

POEMS

AUTONOMEDIA

Thank you to the following people:
Konrad Kleinbub, Madeline Artenberg,
Burton Baroff, Gabriel Don, Jim Feast, Jim Fleming,
Pauline Findlay, Jada Fitzpatrick, Heeyen Park, and
the Fahrenheit Open Mic family.

Thank you to all my teachers along the way
especially Elaine Equi, Barbara Henning,
Jason Schneiderman, Dorianne Laux, Fanny Howe,
Anne Waldman, and Mary Karr.

Very special thank you to Star Black, Phillip Giambri,
and Ron Kolm for their guidance and generosity.

First Printing March 2022
Second Edition 2024
©2024 Linda Kleinbub
All rights reserved.

ISBN: 979-8-9898695-0-3
Library of Congress Control Number: 2024901746

Autonomedia
POB 568 Williamsburg Station
Brooklyn, NY 11211-0568 USA

info@autonomedia.org
www.autonomedia.org

For
Kevin and Nicholas

Acknowledgments

Grateful acknowledgment is made to the editors
of the publications where some of these poems first appeared:

Algebra of Owls: "It Lives in the Basement";
Best American Poetry: "Art"; *Brownstone Poets Anthology:* "Girl
Writing Now"; *CTRL + B The Girls Write Now 2019 Anthology:*
"Relic"; *Eighteen Seventy-Writing from the Fringe:* "Barefoot";
Enizagam Journal: "Awaken"; *First Literary Review East:* "Colors,"
"The Student," "Sunken Ship"; *Forever Night 2017 Anthology:*
"Carnage"; Girls Write Now Voice to Voice 2015 Anthology;
Home Planet News: "Abecedarian Affair," "Markings on the Wall,"
"Painting Demons," "Scratching"; *LiveMag!:* "Friend Request,"
"Suitcase"; *Nassau Poet Laureate Society:* "Be My Garden," "Chores,"
"Everything Old, New Again"; *Nomad's Choir:* "Kaleidoscope,"
"Missing"; *Pa'Lante A La Luz (Charge into the Light) 2018 Anthology:*
"Stumbling"; *Poems About Love and War:* "The Fix," "Greenwich
Village," "She Fell to Earth"; *POSTstranger:* "Nudge"; *The Rainbow
Project:* "Back Road Driving"; *The Razor's Wine (Volumes 1-4):*
"Flying to Lexington While Reading Nick Flynn," "On Horseback,"
"School of Obedience," "Search Muse," "Visibility Unclear";
Riverside Poets: "Beginnings," "Be My Garden," "Brooklyn Botanical
Garden," "Cinquain for Jada," "Pull Me Up," "Spending the Day
with Tinkerbell"; *Sensitive Skin Magazine:* "At the Chelsea," "Cover
Charge," "Sex Pistol"; *Short, Fast and Deadly:* "Wind, Salt and
Seaweed"; *Teflon Feathers and Copper Empathy Rimes of the Ancient
Mariner Yearbook:* "Girl Writing Now"; *Un Bordado De Voces (An
Embroidery Of Voices) 2022 Anthology:* "Friend Request," "Spending
the Day with Tinkerbell" "Beginnings" is a *cento* composed of lines
from W.S. Merwin, Sueyeun Juliette Lee, Mark Doty, Kay Ryan,
Anthony Hecht, Craig Santos Perez, Tim Bowling, W. S. Di Piero,
Gerald Stern, Daniela Gioseffi, Fanny Howe, and Jim Carroll.

...that this is what we sometimes get
if we live long enough. If we are patient
with our lives.
                        — Dorianne Laux
                            "Music in the Morning"

Table of Contents

Canvas, Blank

What we remember
begins with the paint

and the brushes
we choose.

Acrylics, watercolors
all different

some are thick-skinned
others fragile.

Days go by
portraits emerge.

What you thought was invisible
now requires touch.

What you thought you
could accomplish

now requires rain.
Time passes.

If able to start over
how would this river run?

You sew clothing
from candle wicks

light up your creation
paint it while it burns.

Markings on the Wall

Astronomical charts:
born under a moonless sky
cosmos ignited the pyre.
Daddy said it was so hot
Earth could've been on fire.
Funny how we let
ghosts of childhood
hide out in bedroom closets.
Imagination carried us to
Jupiter and beyond. But we
kept
looking over our shoulders.
Marked time on the moon before
night rolled to dawn.
Oxygen in our blood
purple galaxies and meteorites
quench our thirst.
Revolving on this planet
synchronicity brings us
together in one
universe tilting this
vex of harmony.
Weekend warrior extracting
xenon from the night sky
your lantern is fueled by yellow
zinnia flowers.

Visibility Unclear

You wake up blurry count
your blessings saunter around
the kitchen grind beans
try to avoid tripping over cats.
Imagination tumbleweeds,
focus on coffee, toast.

Restless, your mind spins intrigue
that forms fissures of logic,
luxury or torture,
redemption or betrayal,
this solitude
leads to your void.

Chores

After Louise Glück

It's not the rain, I know it.
It's these birds
that make that noise.

I hear them.
That noise does not cease
like your expectations of me:
always wanting more.

That noise
as I go through the motions
on that old bed of ours.

In my head
it's your laundry I do tonight
the heavy load
shoving your soiled garments
into the machine.

Watching the gyrations
your spin cycle.
Oh, those damn birds!
Their caw, caw, caw.

How can I compose myself
in this clamoring silence?

Be My Garden

I need to cleanse myself
dig myself into the dirt
sleep with daffodil bulbs
breathe earth.

I remember where last season's tomatoes grew
where the strawberry patch sent its runners
through the hot peppers and the eggplants.

I need to feel you again
to know you
like I know the dirt in my garden.

I'll rake last season's leaves from you
fertilize you, rejuvenate you.

I want to introduce you
to the praying mantis and the ladybugs
so, they can defend you from parasites.

I want you soil ready
so, I can dig my hands in deep
plant a fragile seedling
water it, watch it grow.

It Lives in the Basement

Loneliness crept up the stairs
stood in a corner
observed the situation
searched for the easiest to infiltrate
curled around her unknown
smoke unseen
loneliness holds her tight
she thinks its warmth is comforting
quickly she's left abandoned,
alone, trying to make snow angels
at midnight.

Awaken

You wake up
in the middle of your life
rain beats against the window.

(shoreline, rocks, balcony, palms)

If time were to stop-
this instant your last
would you know
all elegance created?

Do you understand?
Everything is important?

The bird calls
water whispers morning
this could be your last memory.

Stumbling

Thorns, thistle, be careful baby
that's her heart
soft, wet, fragile.

He looks at her
wanting to eat her up.
She looks delicious, doesn't she?

Vulnerable antique lace
disintegrates easily
his glass shards invisible
pierce her skin, even through
the clothes she wears.

The swallows will still fly
over the blackberry bushes
up into the maples.

She's just a girl with tears in her belly
digging in topsoil, planting deception
linking memoir to history.

Jousting heart,
only she understands this devastation.
Newly slashed her skin pours poison
oily dark
staining sheets infiltrating purity.

Never play games with ornamental lovers.

Art

It was art.
Abstract and alcohol-fueled.

Liquid paint-splattered
graffiti-covered and dangerous.

Surreal.

Savage Beauty of
Alexander McQueen
spray paint guns
aimed at a white dress.

Fragile.

An evening gown
made of peonies and roses
disintegrating.

You said, *Don't write about life
write about art.*

Was it not art?
The finger painting of my hair
the pigment of your eyes
the sculpture of my thigh.

You said, *Don't write about life
write about art.*

Was it not art?
My solo performance
when you left me nude
in the gallery
covered in snow?

At the Chelsea

The cover band plays *Blurred Lines*
beer is cold
skin is tan
far away, my mind writes our story

I'm Nancy Spungen
we grunge around rat-infested subway cars
from CBGB to The Bitter End
we room at The Chelsea

you're crazy man, Sid Vicious
already killing me
still, I open the door
and let you in

Abecedarian Affair

As if it's a dream, she
begins a friendship
cherishes a kiss
dances with smoke rings and fire.
Evenings when the lonely,
fiendish
ghouls in her
head arrive, she becomes a flirt.
Intense conversation-
just a harmless
kiss? Foolishly she
lets him view her vulnerabilities,
memories, sad stories, alone at
night, lusting under the moonlight she
opens her heart
pours out her soul.
Quest to find love,
requires a clear
sound mind, which she gives up
tonight. She remembers a time
under a summer sky a
Valentine love
waltzing on the cliffs of the Heights.
X-rays can't see her open wounds.
Yearning, she paces, a lion caged at the
zoo.

Everything Old, New Again

Late night, city lights
lonely haunts, sticky floors
don't bother us
we grew up
in old New York
with territorial subway rats
whose turf was platforms
not tracks

Today we dine in restaurants
that survived old school city days
we drink in dive bars
cling to a dying past

This night in a reborn Broadway theater
we marvel at chandeliers
and ceiling artwork

We tango past
shell-shocked picture taking tourists
gawking Times Square's blazing lights
stepping as one

out of my element on theater row
my dive bar companion
knows Jimmy's Corner
we squeeze in
raise a glass
clink
we are home

Spending the Day with Tinkerbell

For Gabriel

Journey to Gotham
pixies ride unicorns
to knights in armor
south of the border banquet
we stroll down canyons
under a silver sky
witches' brews and toy stores
selfies with street art
we scatter our dreams on
the Lower East Side

Cinquain for Jada

She wants
to pierce her nose,
I cannot convince her
not to, she is determined, so
we'll go

visit
the East Village,
Whatever Tattoo Shop,
where the Ancient Mariner gets
his ink.

Girl Writing Now

On the L train to Canarsie
she writes lyrics on her forearm
she has no paper.

A bluesy beat cadence
she pens in purple sharpie.
Dreams fall out around her

a homeless guy smiles.
She wears three feathers
in her long dark hair.

With her purr inkwell,
she crafts words for Webster.
She scribes her own saga.

Shooting from this planet
she doesn't need a parachute
she'll loudly leap
and land on her feet.

Text message reads BOOM!
Her reply is:
BOOM before the BOOM!

When she reaches her destination
she gathers her dreams
and allows the homeless guy
to keep the one
he smiled.

Cocktails

Long night at Dada
leaves me with music in my head
after-party at the Bitter End
girlfriends bond over fucked up men.

Cover Charge

Broken souls gather
buy the two-drink minimum,
look for romantic remedies.

Your advice was
Don't write about life
write about art.

I say, *Paint me black*
splatter your pigment
on my wedding dress.

You're a beer-soaked barroom,
I'm an engagement ring
lost on the floor.

You're a smudged Keith Haring drawing.
I'm a boombox missing a beat.
Your kisses were jewels,

dope bought on the Lower East Side.
We crawl out of abandoned squats;
you say you speak fiction —

your heart is exposed,
I tell true stories,
you are forewarned.

The Painter

She paints when her love sleeps.
In darkness, with acrylics on canvas.

She splashes emotions of her temptations,
rinsing her brushes in teardrops,

mixing pigments and heartache.
Moonlight spills through the window;

she turns her sins into painted trees,
hangs them by the desk where she works.

A memory.
She prays in church, forgiveness.

Flowers begin to push up dirt,
instill hope, renewal,

resist going back to darkness.
Turn this day into hope.

Confession does not cure her longings
guided by her harlot heart

she checks her phone messages,
searching for her next paramour.

On Horseback

Bejeweled by the night sky
in sapphire and pearls
I come to you,

a pair of long gloves
keeps me warm —
I wonder what you see.

Do you notice my supple breasts?
My dark mascara, the curve of my neck?
My exposed flesh?

Your eyes cover me
in leopard print
staring with intent.

Fire Burning

I don't want to fight
dismissal can occur.
I come with a white flag
packed away somewhere.
Hudson street is paced in bookstores and bars.

Join me for our evening meal.
Ignite the sparks of future flames.
Can we forget the past, when we were both
emotionally detached?

I order Mexican Cocoa Elixir.
I feel the earth attacking
heart attacking
earthquake and aneurysm,
blood pumps, pounds my heart muscle.

Dividends divided,
cylinders, boxes, set aside.

Imagine we are flying.
Decide the direction of travel.
Everyone wants to see the outcome.

How far have we come?
The light sometimes so blinding
lost in the darkness
we wiggled and squirmed.
Feel the bass pounding.

The vacancy in your chest, the tightening
of your throat, the stop of air,
that was your breath, it's gone.

The pendulum, the ticking beats
wrestling between the sheets
in the still of the moment
of moving speed
follow the sound.

Amazing, as they told you it would
be, filled with trinkets and thistle,
crickets and spider webs.
Decide your fate.
Earth will continue to rotate.

Familiar memories dissolve
gases evaporate intertwine.
Hindsight is 20/20
imagine it so.

Juggling chores and expectations
keep doing what you're doing.

Living in a rat
maze
navigate the sun.

Orion's stars drift
penniless across a
quartz-colored sky.

Rotate with me, we'll
steady each other along
the way. Gravity and
universal pressure,
vows of love that
we confess,

xerox, copy and paste me near
your heart. Listen for my love in
zephyrs floating in the night sky.

Missing

Prell shampoo you
left in my bathroom,
even after I asked you
to take it with you.

I don't know why
I'm telling you this,
now that the green shampoo is gone-

I have to confess,
I saved a lock of your hair
sometimes I take it out
it smells like you.

Greenwich Village

After Louise Glück

Autumn leaves blow gold, rust, and crimson
as a jazz trio plays *Mercy, Mercy, Mercy.*

I met my love under the Brooklyn Bridge
or was it the arch in Washington Square Park?

Did I imagine him?
Did he touch my hair?

I've dealt with nuns
who live in convents.

I've seen children who
jump Double-Dutch.

He squeezed my hand.
Did I dream this?

I drown in my swim.
Is he the reason?

I met my love under the Brooklyn Bridge.
Who is my love?

Disappearing, ice melting,
eclipsed.

Then the subway returned me
to my home, I had forgotten.

Pull Me Up

For Ellen Mandel & Michael Lydon

We'll never be them:
musicians romancing an audience
at Cornelia Street Cafe.

We'll never be that romantic couple
singing in harmony.

You don't play guitar, hardly sing.
I never learned to play piano
only sang in church choir.

All the relationships we've ever had
could never live up to
the handsomest man in the world and his wife:
a man who whistles and plays guitar
while she entices the keyboard, smiling.

They share a magic that we'll never know
a magic that I doubt
we ever felt from any love
we ever knew.

Missed our ship?
Neither lucky enough
to be where we should be.

Back on our little piece of dirt
after a night of heartbreaks
I reach my hand to you.

Will you pull me out of my forsaken garden?
Pull me back into our universe
to that cloud, we survive on?

Pull me up.
I long to see the sun.
Pull me up.

Kaleidoscope

Let color patterns erase your pain.
Crystals turn in a cylinder
mirrored pieces
reflect hues magnified
shapes cast back
shapes transformed
look into the kaleidoscope
look closely

beyond changing color patterns
beyond shifting shapes
beyond tricks of mirrors
look deep, you're changing
colliding into yourself
crashing, trying to
burn your dreams.

Enter the kaleidoscope
turn the cylinder
become enraptured
by colors that twirl.
Do you remember colors?
Colors that move before your eyes
colors you have the power to control.
Can you control this kaleidoscope?

Look up
you hold moonbeams in your fingertips
you control the constellations.
Can you know that?

Sleep in solace this night.
Let color patterns erase your pain.

Odyssey

Late night
iceberg moon

his absence
her aloneness
she wonders

does he search
moonbeams for me?

Is he enticing angels
to sing?

She's a Giant Red star
fading in a Black Hole
untethered in space

a nebula in a
galaxy — lost.

Flying to Lexington Reading Nick Flynn

I can't stop it
Skin will sag
No matter how many squats
All the crunches I do

I float above clouds
Next to me a chubby woman sits
In your seat
Not everyone gets a second chance

I'll check into the hotel alone
I'll search slumber
In the vastness of a king size bed for one

I know it's time for me to travel
You could only carry me
So far

    *

So far
You could only carry me
I know it's time for me to travel

In the vastness of a king size bed for one
I'll search slumber
I'll check into the hotel alone

Not everyone gets a second chance
In your seat
Next to me a chubby woman sits
I float above clouds

All the crunches I do
No matter how many squats
Skin will sag
I can't stop it

The Fix

You're heroin
she's your virgin junkie
euphoria of a first kiss
did it ever exist?

She's an addict
looking for a cure
it was easy for you
to hide the needle
with your charm
crawl into her
in her stupor

dogs bark in her nightmares
on canvas she paints
in navy and black
she awakens in splattered clothing
you destroyed her garden
infiltrated her silence

she was so beautiful once

She Fell to Earth

His lyrics in her brain
create the song
she begins to live,
his chorus
becomes a hangman's noose.

Now a lighted torch
she burns to embers
in a flash,
ashes smoldering
on frozen tundra.

Woman with a kiln
molds pots of clay
fingerless.

Colors

You're blue
I'll pretend I'm yellow
together we'll grow
like green after rain.

Paper Darts

Just beyond them
outside the gallery space
freight trains rumbled and hummed,

cuddled around burning wood
thighs pressed against each other,
orange heat crackled and sparked.

Intoxicated by nature's fumes
she fell in love with a conversation
and a man she will never see again.

Wind, Salt, and Seaweed

a *cento* excerpted from *Tombo*
by W.S. DiPiero

Her bed-messed hair, mango aura,
cherished darkness withdraws into
summer's marbled air.
Behind the clouds, a vortex plunge,
wormy matter, complexifying,
an unfinished squeeze, waiting.

Painting Demons

Late-night she becomes a superhero
surrounded by paints and brushes
reaching out to an artist friend
they cut skin together.

Art is where the soul lives naked.
Words can dance
fool a reader.

In paint, the soul is raw.
Tragedy is thrown on canvas.
Words can't describe it.

Cutting skin releases
intricate, fragile demons,
filled with desire.

Taunting voices permeate his ink
calling her to the edge.
She needs his art.

She will buy tragedy —
intricate, fragile demons,
filled with desire.

Carnage

They sit caddy corner
at the back of the bar
full of poetry and alcohol.

Romantics left empty
share stories, heartache, and anguish.
Raw and honest
hearts exposed, they take turns
slice slivers of heart
place them on the bar.

Tales of a slow death, lasting too long
drama of a love that shattered spirits
mourning a companion lost in a bottle
memoir of a marriage
held together with strings.

They reminisce all night
slice slivers of heart
until the bar is red
covered with blood.

Carnage of lonely souls.
She looks into his blue eyes
revealing behind sorrow, passion.

Words evaporate.
Leaning in she whispers, *Kiss me.*
Lost in each other
for a moment, they are healed.

Is There a Full Moon Tonight?

Kissing again.
Does she think she
can heal herself?

A dog licking his wounds
is distracted from the wonders
of the night sky.

His Muse Wears...

black fringe & sequins
a cabaret can-can girl
his eyes penetrate her
he feels her power
her touch, electric power

He longs to get inside her
to breathe her in
to feel the heat of summer sun

He wants to get quiet with her
to listen to her stories
to understand her sighs

His muse is his drug
his hope   his love
his sex   his hug
his touch   his scent
he wants to score more muse

Nudge

She knows she started this
threw the match on the dryer lint.
She hears their whispers
Look out for that pyromaniac bitch.

Fuel of vodka, pheromones
she becomes slave to skin
tarnished by phantom lures
encircling her.

Is that your wife or another tart?
Interesting juxtaposition.
Dialog of a tainted angel.
Can we please discuss
the etymology of this situation?

School of Obedience

She'll never be Man's Best Friend
Forever she'll remain Pavlov's Dog — in training

He wants her to perform, *Good Dog*
He wants to keep her down, *Bad Dog*

He says *You're so beautiful*
as he strokes her into submission

He knows how to stimulate her
so she does tricks to please him

Still, he rings bells to remind
her of her shortcomings

He tells her *I Love You*
as he hangs wind chimes over her head

Bells ring random in the wind
a haunting melody chimes outside her window

He says *I'm addicted to you*
but she's back in her kennel when he's through

Sometimes he runs his fingers
through the wind chimes

to remind her of her crimes
She knows he is counting her sins

He needs to keep her in her place
keep her down

Sometimes she retreats
Sometimes she hides

She will remain a stray
Still, she scratches at his door

looking for one last bone

Sex Pistol

Some people think gothic means black
the lovers separated
need a good fuck
a partner is out of reach
a dildo can soothe
without warmth, pulse, or heartbeat

Flammable

Rendezvous snafu
gullible girl
naïve minx
she thought
electronic words can create lovers
she prays dear lord her soul to keep

Mercy, Mercy

I heard you hiss it smelled like piss
destroying a friendship facade
was there ever a kiss
I reminisce

memories we hold sacred
so many lies.
Can we forget the anger?
Focus on lips and tongues,
hips, thighs, the strokes inside.

Repeat Offender

It happens after a few drinks
when she lets herself go into that empty space
looking for...
a memory that got away
that hug, that kiss,
reminiscing a scenario
lovers on silkscreen
wet and tumbling
so many positions
better than a game of Twister
she knows he is poison
she knows he is pain
teardrops & hateful words,
he left her bruised
curbside in the rain.
Still, want more?
Girl, do you hear the words
coming out of your mouth?

How to Stop Bad Things

Maybe you have to stop drinking
but maybe not yet
surround yourself with positive energy
Lucille Roberts gym
when you get an artist gig
stay sober
that is the hardest thing
stay sober

Beer Song

I drink so much beer
I disappear

I drive myself into a wall
dancing no, I stumble, I fall.

Can I blame it on the alcohol?

Or is it that while I sleep
I toss and turn, I grind my teeth

is there a solution to be found?
Or am I ready to go underground?

Face the fate
let the levy break

all the memories
I isolate.

No one wants to live
underground.

I drink so much beer
I disappear

I cannot dance
I stumble, I fall.

I blame it on the alcohol.

Yaddo Gardens

Marble arch, steel gates
gushing fountains drown out
the highway's hum.

Oasis where nude lovers are turned to stone
ferns hold artists' ambition
in the summer wind.

Rock formations cover indecency
the fragrance of roses, water flows
cleansing shortcomings.

Shady lair strengthened by pearl columns.
Cumulous clouds
play tag as they drift above.

I drop my thoughts to the koi
swimming in their orange and ebony suits.
Transformed, I return to the place

where wages are made on ponies
and dreams die by a nose.
For a moment
I was pure.

Back Road Driving

Back road driving
in the evergreens
can lead to quiet streams

keep holding telescopes
star searching
orange in the sunset still visible

lay beside me longer
tangled limbs
branches in the backyard

Web

The tangled web of life starts small
we spin our silk of tender thread
with strength to capture
hornets and gypsy moths
web grows
if undisturbed

Fog on Your Eyelashes

Slow down baby
you're running on empty,

flash dance chaos
floats cumulous, then gone.

You are drowning in
verbs and highlights.

Buried trauma: a sleeping cat
curled up in the crawlspace of your brain.

A friend recommends therapy
you won't play that game.

Your smoke is disintegrating
your mirrors are cracked.

Reaching for comets
your fireworks are burned.

Time to pack up your crazy
put on your clothes

fix your eyebrows
your lipstick

kaleidoscope like
nobody knows.

Friendly Competition

I remember the games we played:
Strip Poker, Twister, and Life
but soon we became
Knock um Sock um robots
and Battleship ruled the course.

You were Nok hockey
I was looking for Barbie's dream house.
I was just trying to Connect
but you Scrabbled my heart.

Our Mystery Date soon became a Charade
you Boggled my mind
our love was Taboo
you left me without a Clue.

You were an action figure
I was a paper doll.
It was supposed to be a quick
game of Blackjack
but life is a slow-moving chess game.
The next move is yours.

Friend Request

Politics on Facebook
filled with manipulation and lies
I can't play that game.
This public display
show what you please,
fill your world with pretty pictures
or try to cure a disease.
Did somebody say
"Birthday Fundraiser Please?"
It's the Facebook parade.

Self-promotion free of charge.
Who's in charge?
You can show me your nightmare
or put on a show,
become a fantasy lover
who's to know?
Guaranteed personality upgrade.
What? Now you want to unfriend me?
What a tease!

Droid

Don't bother me phone
let me do my work
I mute you, still, you vibrate
rattle on that little table
don't talk to me phone
no more Instagram
no more Facebook
no more Twitter
no more TikTok

you connect me to strangers in strange places
you're my art museum, my new love interest
a card game that leaves me in solitude

go away phone
you make me forget my closest friends
your texting reply bubbles
are ruining my relationships
Internet that connects the universe
Internet that leads me astray
Internet filled with ISIS recruiters
and poetry brothels

don't hum, don't bing, don't buzz phone
leave me alone phone
let me get my job done
begin my journey in the sun
relax in my skin
when evening begins
and fireflies take flight
I'll shimmy in the starlight

Locket

Embroidery
Crucifix
Burning
Impenetrable
Metropolitan
Mediterranean
Poem for Jim Carroll
Lorca
Pink blossoms hung from trees
Myself unfolding
Through a microscopic lens
Speak the language
Your cha cha
Your rumba
Complete unpretentiousness
Willem de Kooning
Taxi ride
Capable
Judgment
Lazy birds
Styrofoam
Paper bags
Idolized

Detonate

A conversation full of color
embarks on the journey

flowers blossom
botanic radiance

vibrant blue, half-memories
your body strong, sublime & gorgeous

life, as it flows, begins with love
tunneling inward, your bareback, tan stomach

fearlessness to follow pleasure
connection in the burning rhythm

magnificent lyrical sequences
your bare shoulders, behold a space in which

Earth's orbit burns; patterns scattered
all into focus surrounded by
                                        a whisper.

Barefoot

We walk a million miles
from Santa Fe
our imagination
steel buckets crammed
with Dixieland Jazz.

Metals bright and dark
absorbed by jewels
aglow in the Appalachian Forest.

Floating on Tugaloo River
a long wooden boat
with captivating designs
looks dangerous
stark and mystical.

Out of thin air, an
apricot ribbon
ruffles the night sky
elegant reason
for my invitation.

Everyone's dancing.

Later it rains
kerosene.

Relic

We rush about gathering pages.
What colorful lament leaves regret?

Leaves, we've meant to photograph,
we gaze up looking for stars
building the sun.

The equality of secrets,
secrets positioned,
pruned and tied neatly along the fence.

Task at hand becomes a distraction:
phone calls unanswered,
voices unheard,
messages unread.

Is there serenity in the steps you shuffle?

And what comes of the pages?
Myths of scorn and greed
blanketed in the silence of memory lost.

We return again to meditate
as we move along underground tracks
through underwater tunnels.

We gather again.

A scrap of ideas,
a phrase of prayer,
a creation, we made.
Our ancestor's assignment remembered.

What will be remembered?
In this rhythm beaten down
generations lost,
a faded photograph
only to be slipped between pages,
folded to form book,

book to be passed on
to future relations
still unknown,
still unconceived.

Held on by tradition.
Held on by a string.
Held on until your grasp fails.

Let go.

Are we left empty-handed?
What imprint in the dust?

Brooklyn Botanical Garden

For Madeline

One day I'll look at these photographs
yellow narcissus and pink Japanese cherry
see our smiling faces

I'll forget how drained
how tense I was
I'll remember the day

woman writers bonded as they marveled
the delicate white flowers
of the paperbush.

Choices

People who dwell over life choices
regret their own life choices
need to realize
that every day they wake up
they are faced with new choices.

If you're not satisfied,
still dreaming
wake up tomorrow,
and make new choices.

Search Muse

My head is heavy and my hands are dry.
My muse wanders in my neighbor's yard
breathing in the midnight air
all I can do is watch her
chase lightning bugs.

I left myself somewhere
while gathering chores
trying to find
missing puzzle pieces.

Did I place myself upon a shelf
sometime while tidying up
the junk mail and magazines?

Where is my muse?
Is she lurking under sofa cushions
where my cats perch
ready to pounce prey?

Pretend we don't have time to squander
hold me close, I need you near me now
please touch me.

My muse comes in the quiet peeling
of a second clementine, my tongue
still tingles citrus.

I put the kettle on
to take the chill out of the room.
I entice my muse late-night with candlelight.

Chamomile steeps,
she whispers, *Patience.*

Riptide

She breathes poetry
from Rockaway's surf
broken by waves
beach bonfire chaos
sandcastle's starfish
this driftwood, her poison
asleep on the sand
she washes out to sea.

The Student

Ink strokes form letters
letters form words
arranged in an order
to form sentences
mark this time on earth.
Poet, what song do you sing?
How do you present your imagination?

I'm studying toe stretching.
I've got so much time on my hands.

Scratching

You've been raking on my mind again
scratching at my nerves
time to clear the twigs and branches
I've been raking over you
scratch, scratch, scratch
pull and tug
smack and pull
smack and tug

Trailer Trash

you crawl out of the shadows
late night
after the game
when you are buzzed
alone in your double trailer
when your dog isn't enough company
you pick up your phone
and message me "Yo"

The Hangover

Don't tempt her, fragile heart
she is loved, yet still seeks sin

never satiated, always thirsty.
Under the blood-red moon

playing with a string of loves
whole heart testimonies

her mouth moves
unaware of consequences.

As night fades, daylight illuminates
the mess she made.

Sunken Ship

fog made of salt
tears of mermaids

voices rising from deepest sorrow
carry me towards daylight

fuse myself whole again
wipe my tears with beach fire coals

lose me on the shoreline
let me become food for seagulls

Observation

The man in the moon is watching the night
Jupiter and Saturn are in view.

Midnight sky sings a cricket chorus.
My wonder is filled with worry for you.

This night of solitude,
a soothing tune, a calming rhythm

the neighbor's pool filter bubbles and hums.
Struggles within, jousting emotions

dueling against oneself.
Underlying conditions need to be examined.

Energy in the spectrum —
a whirly-gig spinning on a slippery surface.

Her Gardener

Allured by pheromones
he cultivates flowers
poppies, begonias, lily of the valley.

Tonight, she waits for him in her garden
surrounded by seedlings, star searching.
He's exhausted
tending to his narcissus tonight.

Still, she waits watching
vegetables grow in darkness
hoping he will come around
tend to his rose
remove the weight of dead branches.

Her roots are deep but she's been harmed
by ice storms that came late spring.

Two-stepping into Infinity

This day together
could be our last day together

hold my hand, stay close.
Let's hope we get lucky

and we get tomorrow
a new day.

This step could be the last step
for both of us.

Wrong place, wrong time
we could two-step into infinity.

Hold my hand, stay close.
I want to spend

another day
with you.

Beginnings

a cento

Unseen by each other we have been transformed
and the contradictions that emerge
that hold the world in place
abstracts you and in some way, from nature.

You stand in this morning's shadows
more common than wind.
It is time to be thankful for the breath
we feel somehow between us.

Now is the mourning of that day
we will live in the light
like the genius of flowers
known only to few, in certain high mountains.

Suitcase

In the quiet time of evening
when the katydid's song ends
the moon still shines above.

She's packing her suitcase
what will she carry home?

Under the silent stars
investments made in
time multiply or they

can disintegrate by
astronomical charts
sent via email.

Everyone knows
you need to look up
to see the galaxy.

About the Author

Linda Kleinbub's family settled on 12th Street and Avenue B on New York's Lower East Side when they arrived from Poland at the turn of the century. She is a lifelong Queens resident. She returned to the land of her ancestors as a photographer in the early eighties, capturing the abandoned tenements and desolate city streets. Later as an MFA candidate at the New School, she immersed herself into the downtown poetry scene. She is curator and host of Fahrenheit Open Mic and founder of Pen Pal Poets. She's the publisher and editor of *The Silver Tongued Devil Anthology* (Pink Trees Press, 2020.) Linda was one of six local poets invited to read at the Americas Poetry Festival of New York 2021. She's hosted readings at the Playhouse Theater, New York City Poetry Festival, 6BC Botanical Garden, and Black & White Bar. Follow her on Instagram @LINDAKLEINBUB to see some of her published work. This is her first full-length book of poetry.